EXPERIENCE
ENGINES

WARNING

Do **not** stop now
Do **not** look up
Do **not** listen further

Do **not** speak
Do **not** ask
Do **not** question

Do **not** see
Do **not** imagine
Do **not** understand

Do **not** think
Do **not** wonder
Do **not** refuse

Do **not** turn
Do **not** worry
Do **not** change

Do **not** do this
Do **not** do that
Do **not** do nothing

Do **not** do anything
Do **not** do now
Do **not** now stop

EXPERIENCE ENGINES

JAMIE INGLIS

Contact the author
info@jamieinglis.com

Many thanks to **Alex Nisbet** for kind permission to reproduce
'Lilies, Edinburgh' on the front cover, *'Burning the Page #1'* on the
back cover and *'Burning the Page #2'* on page 94.
www.alexnisbet.com

Hubble telescope images: facing page 1 and page 56 © NASA/JPL.
All photographs and other images © Jamie Inglis 2010.

Burning the Page - from Paper to Pixel.   www.burningthepage.com
The Science Fiction Index - The best of all time.   www.sci-fi-index.com
New Neologisms - new words for new times.   www.newneologisms.com
The Poetry Index - the finest poets and poetry.   www.poetry-index.com
The Disorganised Society - real life is disorganised.   www.disorganised.org

Printed by Lulu
www.lulu.com/content/7586692

Published by
PROHIBITED PUBLICATIONS
79 Bruntsfield Place
Edinburgh
EH1O 4HG
Scotland
www.prohibitedpublications.com

PP Prohibited Publications
ISBN 978-0-9556810-9-7

9 780955 681097

By the same author

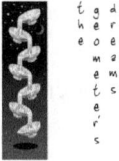

the geometer's dreams   (1992)

fractals & mnemonics   (1996)

hold on   (2000)

gluon notes   (2006)

collected poems 1985 - 1999
(2009)

Experience Engines
Jamie Inglis
First Edition Paperback © 2010

Experience Engines is the fifth collection of poems
by Jamie Inglis. It includes a handful of favourites from his
fourth collection, *Gluon Notes* followed by six sets of new poems
including; some Start Engines, travel notes, more poems
from a frontline living room, poems for tomorrow,
new Scottish Politics and Scottish haiku's
and a few more New Neologisms.

Poems about travelling near and far, of times, places
and who we are. Poems about the unexpected and
unexplained and about wars fought in our name.
Poems of new words embedded in the web.

Jamie Inglis is a poet and doctor from Edinburgh.
He has worked and published on a wide range of
public health issues including HIV, cancer, immunisation, tobacco,
drugs, obesity and others.
He had his first poems published aged ten and after qualifying in
medicine returned to writing poetry in the 1980's.
His poems reflect his interests in pacifism, travel, sci-fi,
the world we live in and the world we are creating.
After travelling round the world three times
he lives in Edinburgh.

EXPERIENCE ENGINES

Previously - *Gluon Notes*

Start Engines

Travel Notes

from a frontline living room

Tomorrow

New Scottish Politics

Scottish Haiku's

more New Neologisms

colophons

Previously

gluon notes

jamie inglis

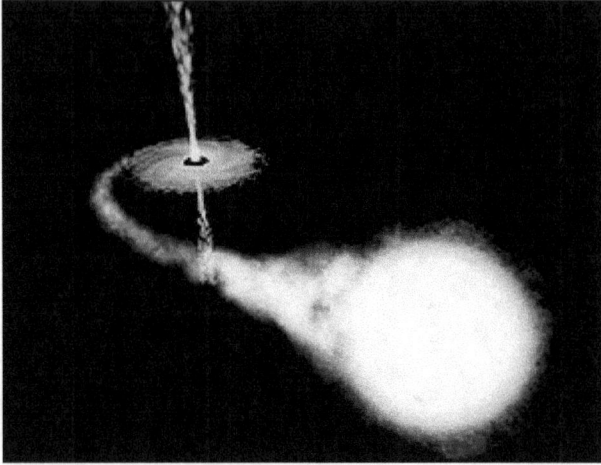

Black hole passing a star   (© NASA/JPL)

Gluon Note

Give me time
and I will take you anywhere.
Give me a second
and I will take you to a star.

Give me time
and I will make you anywhere.
Give me a lifetime
and I will make you a star.

Gluon

There are eight different types of gluon: they have no mass, travel at the speed of light and have colour and anti-colour.

Oxford Paperback Encyclopaedia, © *Oxford University Press 1998*

Dream night

Maybe tonight
is a dream night
something to remember, for tomorrow.

Maybe tonight
is a silent night
nothing to remember, if this is tomorrow.

Maybe tonight
is another night
everything remembered, it is tomorrow.

Warriors of Xian

Acres of soldiers
arrayed in square fields
standing, made from clay.

Cavalrymen and horses
eerily silent
in the red earth.

A motionless army
still for centuries
waiting the millennia away.

A tomb of terracotta,
legions of patient warriors
waiting through eternity.

Warriors of Xian
guarding forever
The Emperor's future.

Wreath Street, Hanoi

For Boa Ninh (2)

Wait for me here
until forever.

Wait for me here
until after forever.

Wait for me here
until forever has passed.

Wait for me here
make me be here.

Armistice morning, Saint-Nazaire 11.11.00

Armistice morning, Saint-Nazaire 11.11.00

At eleven 'o' clock
the old men wearing their medals
and the standard bearers and the band
gather with fanfare
at the monument des morts.

More medals are presented.
Brave speeches are made
to remember those who are dead.

The wreaths are laid.
The standards are lowered
and a hundred doves take to the air.

The band form up
and the old soldiers behind
march off with their memories.

One hundred yards down the quayside
the Monument des Commandos is quiet
no flags, no ceremony today.

A Year of Rubble

After the first hour
of the first war
of the twenty-first century.

There was a year
of rubble and bodies
from the first hour of the terror war.

After the first hour
of the first move
there were pieces all over the world.

After the first hour
we could stand no more
and the waiting started
for the end of the war.

War Day Three

War Day Three
and now years of war lie ahead.
Only the tears of Allah
and all his followers
will satisfy the US.

War Day Three
more countries at war lie ahead.
Collapsing and imploding
till Islam is revealed
will satisfy the US.

War Day Three
deaths every day in the war ahead.
Only the tears of Allah
and all his followers
will satisfy the US.

Speaking as friends

Speak to me as a friend
and treat me as someone you have just met.

We should have no secrets
and your body should tell me no lies.

Tell me only your truest thoughts
that only a stranger should ever hear.

Start Engines

The page that was never there

You won't find it here.
You won't find it there.
The page is everywhere.

You won't find it here.
You won't find it anywhere.
Your page is everywhere.

You won't find it here.
You'll never find it now.
The page was never there.

A Thread Understood
'Pattern Recognition'

A pattern brought to life
before your blinkered eyes.

A pattern exposed to light
the ideas shining ever brighter.

A thread unravelled
to be better understood.

A thread understood
a threat laid to rest.

Three friends well known

Here, there and far
three friends well met.
Here, there and far.

Start, travel and destination
here, there and far.
Cycle, life and death.

Here, there and far
three friends well known.
Here, there and far.

The Pointless Club

All the streets are numbered there,
somewhere between heaven and here.
Long passageways full of secret keys.
A lost island locked in the trees.

All the avenues are numbered there,
some oasis that we all share.
Beyond the maze that is despair,
life's utopia for all to compare.

All the roads are numbered there,
somewhere between heaven and here.
Many crossroads full of hidden signs,
our island, always our times.

The Age of Pessimism

The Age of Pessimism
and Generation X.

The baby-boomers
become grumpy old men.

Generation X inherit
and do not care.

So few have hope
the rest despair.

A life of dreams

We live a life of dreams.
Dreams of ourselves, dreams of others.

A life full of dreams.
Dreams of people, dreams of places.

A full life of dreams.
Dreamed by ourselves, not by others.

You are my world

You are my world,
all of it, and nothing less.

You are all my world,
all of you, and nothing less.

You will be my world,
all of time, and nothing less.

Hot and Cold Conundrum

Hot taps on the left, cold taps on the right.
No, cold on the left, hot on the right.
No, that can't be right,
cold is on the right.

There must be a rule to get it right
but is it hot or cold on the right.

Select Society 2

Deselected from The Select Society.
Standing outside The Inner Circle.
Reselected for The Select Society.
Stepping inside The Inner Circle.

Life in and out of Lots of Societies.
Inside and out of All the Circles.
Death inside Some of these Societies.
Stuck within One of the Circles.

Faith in You

Do not put your faith in one belief.
Do not put your faith in one religion.
Do not put your faith in one belief system.

Do not put your faith in one belief.
Do not put your faith in world peace.
Do not put your faith in human nature.

Put your faith in your belief.
Put your faith in your conviction.
Put your faith in you.

Do not save the best for last

Do not save the best for last.
Now is the best.

Do not ask
how long will it last?

Longer than this moment
has taken to pass.

Living long enough to understand locks

Locks on our doors,
locks on our secrets,
all of us prone to deceit.

Doubts of our security,
doubts of our exposure,
all of us prone to doubt.

Some doors are secure,
some secrets are safe,
all of us prone to doubt.

Living long enough to understand,
locks are always open,
with those you truly trust.

Its easy to remember

Love at first sight
its easy to remember.
I did not put up a fight
its easy to remember.

Love at first sight
its easy to remember.
It was now and right
its easy to remember.

Love at first sight
its easy to remember.
Lying awake through the night
its easy to remember.

Love at first sight
its easy to remember.
Forever in my sight
no need to remember.

Travel Notes

Isla de Ometepe, Lago de Nicaragua

Titanic Cemetery, Halifax, Nova Scotia

The Lost Half Hour
Flying to Canada and back

London to St. John's,
    four hours back.

St. John's to Halifax,
    a half hour back.

Halifax to London,
    four hours forward.

That lost half hour,
    where is it now?

Links Twilight

Walking into the sunlight
out of the first shadow of the day.

A shard of light
preceding the dark across the face of day.

A ray remains in sight
dividing the shadow at the end of the day.

Then comes night
lit by artificial suns turning night to halogen day.

Touching the Fire Dragon

Perched on the caldera's rim.
A rumble builds beneath your feet
and blows the explosion through your soles.
Add deafening sound and the caldera erupts.
Throwing tons of lava and rocks towards the clouds.
A molten river rising before your eyes
and turning and raining back down below your feet.
A seering red retinal streak.
Touched, the Fire Dragon.

Mr CIA Man on the ferry to New Amsterdam

New Amsterdam ferry with Mr CIA.
A lie from the first about crossing from Suriname.

Investigating murders in these here parts.
Superintendent killed was it that?
New York City cop now working for Justice.
A reconnaissance of possible hostile.
We're on holiday no knowledge of murders.
From Scotland, not Irish and IRA.

The ferry started loading, Mr CIA to his armour.
Only gates were opening still time to wonder.
No cars were moving yet Mr CIA.
Only people from everywhere crossing over today.

Mr CIA doesn't know the length of the crossing.
I speak politely to people passing. Thirty minutes.
Going back to speak to Mr CIA alarms the spooks.
Set Mr CIA on edge for thirty entertaining minutes.

An unknown quantity relaxing and smoking on the ferry.

To New Amsterdam with Mr CIA.

With armoured 4x4, partner and locals.

Still not Irish, no thanks to a guiness.

Water on the ferry to New Amsterdam courtesy of Mr CIA.

Happy to banter with locals, joking and in your face.

Wary of inconsistencies is the unknown stranger.

Watching Mr CIA wonder on the ferry to New Amsterdam.

As you travel more

As you travel more.
More cities, lands and people
are part of your world.

As you travel more.
More cities, lands and people
are devastated in your wake.

As you travel more.
The world's cities, lands and people
are preparing for their own storm.

As you travel more.
To the world's cities, lands and people
are we not masters of our future.

As you travel more.
You become sensitised
to the world's disasters.

A tsunami here,
a bomb there,

a hurricane somewhere else,
a hostage crisis again.

In an age of global media
for most a faraway disaster.
No connectedness,
to events unfolding.

For many each disaster
will be personal.
For a few, most disasters
will be personal.

As you travel more,
in our time of disaster and terror.
The cities, lands and people
are changing and uniting,
and these voices will be heard.

Los Almendros de San Lorenzo

(not the only gay in the village)

Los Almendros de San Lorenzo
made a fine mojito, the best in Suchitoto.
A gay Parisian boutique hotel in Suchitoto,
the poorer lover manages the business.
Now a big new hotel overlooking the square
a gay Spaniard runs with his secret
Salvadorian business lover.
Frisson for the only gay loses its savour.
Suchitoto now has a gay community
always at each others throats.
The flavour of unique has been lost to normality.
The new gays take their profit
and retire to the coast.
Parisian and partner left behind.

The Beach at Wikiki

Walking the beach at Wikiki.
Diamond Head brooding at our back.
Browning bodies bake prone on the sand
waves roll through thousands in the sea.
Foaming at the waterline, a scum of factor
reflecting oil slicks on the surface of the sea.
Through a sinking sunset watched
mostly by silent American and Japanese eyes
from countless cocktail bars and grills.
The towering concrete of rooms and suites behind
encasing the dream of the beach at Wikiki.

In Paris, waiting for the tour

In Paris, waiting for the tour to arrive.
Preparing for the peleton
or the breakaway on the Champs-Elysee.
Glory before the Arc in a couple of days.

In Paris, two days before the tour.
A Friday, the holidays start today.
By Monday, all of Paris will be away.
On Sunday, all stand to hail the tour.

Kaiteur Falls, Republic of Guyana

Disorganised at Kaiteur, © Alison Boyd

from a frontline living room

Saddam in their sights

How many more nights
of Saddam in their sights
before somebody blinks
and out go the lights.

Second attack inevitable

20.05.02
Six months into The War on Terror
the US warns a Second attack is inevitable.

The next attack is coming.
Al-Queda are preparing
their second attack.

This war is far from over.
This war is far from won.

One attack behind us.
How many more to come?

Wednesday 29th May 2002

Wednesday 29th May 2002.
Last day of clearing-up Ground Zero.
Last piece of wreckage removed.
Last steel girder cut down
wrapped in a shroud
and borne aloft
to leave Ground Zero
and the final ceremony tomorrow.

11 Months After

Now 40 US soldiers dead
11 months after 9/11.

Hundreds or thousands of Afghan dead
11 months after 9/11.

Hundreds or thousands more around the world
11 months after 9/11.

Hundreds or thousands or many more to die
In The War on Terror after 9/11.

Bombs in Bali

Bombs in Bali
Bombs in paradise.

Bombs in Benidorm
Bombs in Belfast.

Bombs in Bali
A hole in the heart of paradise.

Bombs in Bali
Warchalk another hole in our hearts.

10/12 Bali

Bombs explode
fifteen and twenty years in my past
and resonate through the years.

Bombs in paradise
not as I remember it
but in a western theme park paradise.

Bombs in western paradise
the second front of dreaded terror.
Next Disneyland and Uncle Sam.

Bombs on 9/11, 10/12.
The anniversaries begin to coincide
in a forever war for both sides.

Gulf War II

On the brink
of Gulf War II.
This month, March
they say for sure.

On the brink
of a war without frontiers.
This month, forever
our world will change.

A Minute to Midnight

A minute to midnight
to invade Iraq.

A minute to midnight
how will they fight back.

A minute to midnight
why do we attack?

A minute to midnight
Invasion Iraq.

A minute to midnight
not to late to turn back.

A minute to midnight
and the start of the flack.

A minute to midnight
standby Iraq.

A minute to midnight
Goodbye Iraq.

Five years on
12th September 2006

Five years on, year one,
The War on Terror goes on.

Five years on, year two,
The War goes on and on.

Five years on, year three,
how long will this go on?

Five years on, year four,
who knows when this will stop?

Five years on, year five and counting,
who knows how this will end?

Las Malvinas War Memorial, Buenos Aires

The last war we fought on our own

Twenty-five years after Gotcha
modest remembrance of the end of empire.
One thousand deaths in a short war
for our Falkland Overseas Territories.

Twenty-five years after the Belgrano,
Sheffield, Sir Galahad, Atlantic Conveyer and more.
To watery graves in the South Atlantic
and barren hillside graves, in the South Atlantic.

Twenty-five years after hostilities
only we and Argentina remember.
Would we act the same today
for our Falkland Overseas Territories?

Every step
(between the trenches)

Each step gets harder here
in no-mans land
between the fire.

Each step in no-mans land
between the fire
gets harder here.

Each step between the fire
gets harder here
in no-mans land.

Tomorrow

Hubble Ultra Deep Field (© NASA/JPL)

When the final night falls

To be with you
when the stars fall.

To be with you
when the stars fall from the sky.

To be with you
when the last night falls.

To be with you
when darkness falls.

To be with you
when the final night falls.

Fast Anaesthetisers

Hard to say, easy to not notice.
Those fast aneasthetisers
we meet every day.

Fast aneasthetisers, from TV to soap.
Infoporn on the infoban
pervading our lives.

Fast aneasthtisers, go digital at night.
Pixels and gigabytes
capturing our lives.

Fractal String

Bloodhound String
kernal 386.exe

Live the world
Be the world
Live the web
Worldweb
Join the world
Join the worldweb
Run the world
Who runs the web
Whose in charge
Whose in charge here
No-one's in charge
No-one's in charge now
We run the world
This is how the world runs
This is how the web runs
This is how the web works
We fix your organisation
We run the worldweb
We run the web
We run the world

Poem for Search Engines

[128 bit unencrypted poem]

Poem, poem, poem, poem.
Poem, poem, poem, poem.

Poem, poem, poem, poem.
Poem, poem, poem, poem.

Poem, poem, poem, poem.
Poem, poem, poem, poem.

Poem, poem, poem, poem.
Poem, poem, poem, poem.

The C Library

If disaster strikes
and there are no more books
at least you will have
those you own.

If disaster strikes again
and books are to valuable to be lent
only your own to read again.
Not with a Classic Library.

I will be me again

I will be me again
no matter what they take.
I will be I again
whatever I should lose.

It will still be me
after their damage is done.
It will still be I
when loss has turned to gain.

One event

Now, in our time
one event
can change the world in a day.

Throughout time
one event
could change your world in a day.

Before our time
one event
could not change the world in a day.

Anytime now
one event
could change the world in a day.

In our time
one event
will change the world in a day.

VCR Dementia

Blank technology spots

Areas of electronic darkness

Gaps of information understanding

Data loss on the highway

Missing facets of function

Advancing areas of noise

Blank knowledge spots

Blank spots

Blank

.

Future History

Strong common history
binds our lives together.
Mirror image roots
shaped throughout our childhood.

Early years encircling
ties our current life.
Shared years of growing
towards our common future.

Large Hadron Collider

Hadrons collide at the start of time.
From nothing, something leads to everything.

Looking at light from the dawn of time.
Nothing familiar in the Ultra Deep Field.

Emergent Functions

The mathematics of Emergent Functions.
Space outwith our own geometry's.
Worlds without number at every junction.
Life unique in all these universes.

We are the Emergent Function.

Tomorrow's a bonus

Not this yet
will become it
only after time.

Not this yet
but will become it
after time has passed.

New Scottish Politics

MSP's Offices, Scottish Parliament, Edinburgh

Three men, two dead to blame

A Scottish Parliament is built
[Three men, two dead to blame].

The architect - Enric Miralles
for designing such an expensive building.

The First Minister - Donald Dewar
for approving the building.

The Presiding Officer - Lord [call me Sir David] Steel
for dithering about the building.

Cost £500 Million.

One week away

In the week we were away
The Scottish Parliament became
what it was always destined to be
the very finest operatic comedie.

A Lord MSP sets fire to curtains.
The Scottish Socialists expel their founder.
What further entertainment awaits us?
A bargain at £500 million pounds

Five AM Election Night 2007

Selotape democracy in Edinburgh West

6.9% swing to SNP in First Minister Jack's Wishaw

3.7% of ballots spoilt, almost 1,000 votes

Arran's votes stalled at sea

       The island's helicopter grounded

Anniesland thickiesland with 1,700 spoilt ballots [7.2%]

Only 5 results by 2AM

Dundee the first Nationalist City

Ballieston thickiston with 1,850 spoilt ballots

Shettleston superthickiston with 2,050 ? spoilt, turnout 33%

4.30AM, 41 seats in, count abandoned at Strathkelvin

then elsewhere,

and here.

The 10% Democracy?

The 20% Democracy.

What led us here?

50% of people vote,

40% of these elect a Government,

equals one in five of the population.

80% voted for someone else

    or not at all.

National Governments no longer represent.

Local Councils are already at 15% Democracy.

In another ten years.

The 10% Democracy?

Our first constitutional crisis

One month after the historic Scots election
our first constitutional crisis appears.
A memorandum in a tent with the Libyan nation
has Scotland's First Minister the happiest in years.

Edinburgh's G8 moment

And yet, somehow now
the world turns and watches
Edinburgh, Scotland
awaiting its G8 moment.

Dreams of Enlightenment days past.
Dreams of poverty in the past.
Nightmares of the world unlocked at last.

And yes, this is now
our moment has come at last.
All our voices will be heard
filling the G8 moment.

And yes, our now
will be with the world watching.
Turning our dreams to dust or light.
And you? In your G8 moment.

Wha's for a dram?

Give me a splash
in the bottom of the glass.
No, that can't be right
it doesn't rhyme.

Give me a dash
in the bottom of the glass.
No, no right either
still doesn't rhyme.

Give me a dram
that's Scotland's dwam.

Scottish Haiku's

White Peacock, Funchal Botanical Gardens, Madeira

Knowledge Haiku

Walking in new directions
with no knowledge of before.

Walking in different directions
before the knowledge goes.

Haiku for Lonely Planet

For some it is the travel path.
For some it is the aftermath.

Crowd Cloud

I watched a crowd go by
and watched a friend pass me by.

I watched a cloud go by
and watched it stare me in the eye.

The Complete Citizen

50% Socialist, of course.
25% Nationalist, naturally.
25% Anarchist, who me?

Do it again

Do it again
Don't do this again
Don't do it
Don't do this
Do it like this
Don't do it like this
Don't do it again

Its happening again

Where in time

Time is also a where.
Now is somewhere in time.

This where in time
is now.

Only memories are left
as dreams of then.

Hanging Dante, Prvic Luka, Croatia

78

What lies ahead is already here

What's ahead of us
is here now.
If we could see
the sparks here and now,
the time ahead of us
would be visible now.

RLS was wrong

Someone to love.
Someone who loves you.
Somewhere to belong.
Somewhere to hope for.

Unexpected Life

Just because it happens
doesn't mean
    you have to go looking for it.

The Human Quandary

The outward and inward urges.
Forever forward and beckoning back.

Drawing us on and back within.
Holding us hypnotised and promising us peace.

Concrete Hellfire

Religion is conviction without evidence.

Evidence is the religion of conviction.

Conviction is the evidence of religion.

Friendship Haiku

Friendship always (usually) survives honesty

but very rarely lies.

Waiting Game

Steady waiting game, to prevent your gain,
holding on, taking the strain.
Quarter, quatrain, its only a game,
nothing ever stays the same.

more

New Neologisms

www.NewNeologisms.com

RUNCHAOS

Initiate each unstable event chain,
leading to chaos who knows when.

Initiate every unstable event chain,
leading to chaos here, there and everywhen.

www.runchaos.com

TIMEDART

A pierced moment from the past,
flies through time designed to last.

A memory arrow from the past,
strikes through reality outwith our grasp.

www.timedart.com

TEXTEXIT

Final words written saved and sent,
before your eyes and in your mind.

Final words written before getting bent,
adverts, clicks and sales pay the rent mind.

www.textexit.com

E-MEMES

Electronic ideas spreading through cyberspace,
as a storm of microscopic motes.

Electronic ideas spreading through the human race,
inside a cloud of driven nanobots.

www.e-memes.com

DONOINFO

Avoiding information trails in data hungry devices,
invisible steps at the machine interface.

Outside the information track in memory hungry mainframes,
silent footsteps passing without leaving a trace.

www.donoinfo.com

EMITTIME

Time backwards and time forward.
Backwards time and forward time.

Living within the flow of time.
Creating time from the mirror.

www.emittime.com

Colophons

Just Starting

Sometimes we think
we have been everywhere,
we have seen everything.
But mostly I think
if I had a thousand years
I would only just be starting.

End of the day poem of the leftover words

When you write a few words
and give them away
they are lost forever
those words you wrote
that day.

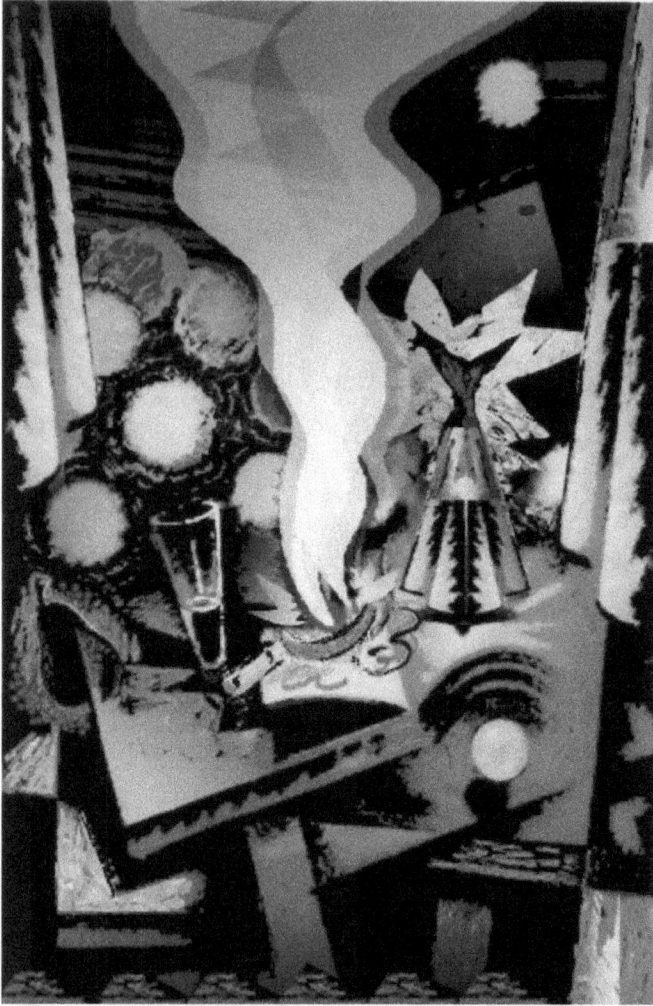

Burning the Page #2, Alex Nisbet

PP Prohibited Publications
ISBN 978-0-9556810-9-7

吉米·因够斯医生

Newton, *Sir Eduardo Paolozzi, Dean Gallery, Edinburgh*

e-experience engines

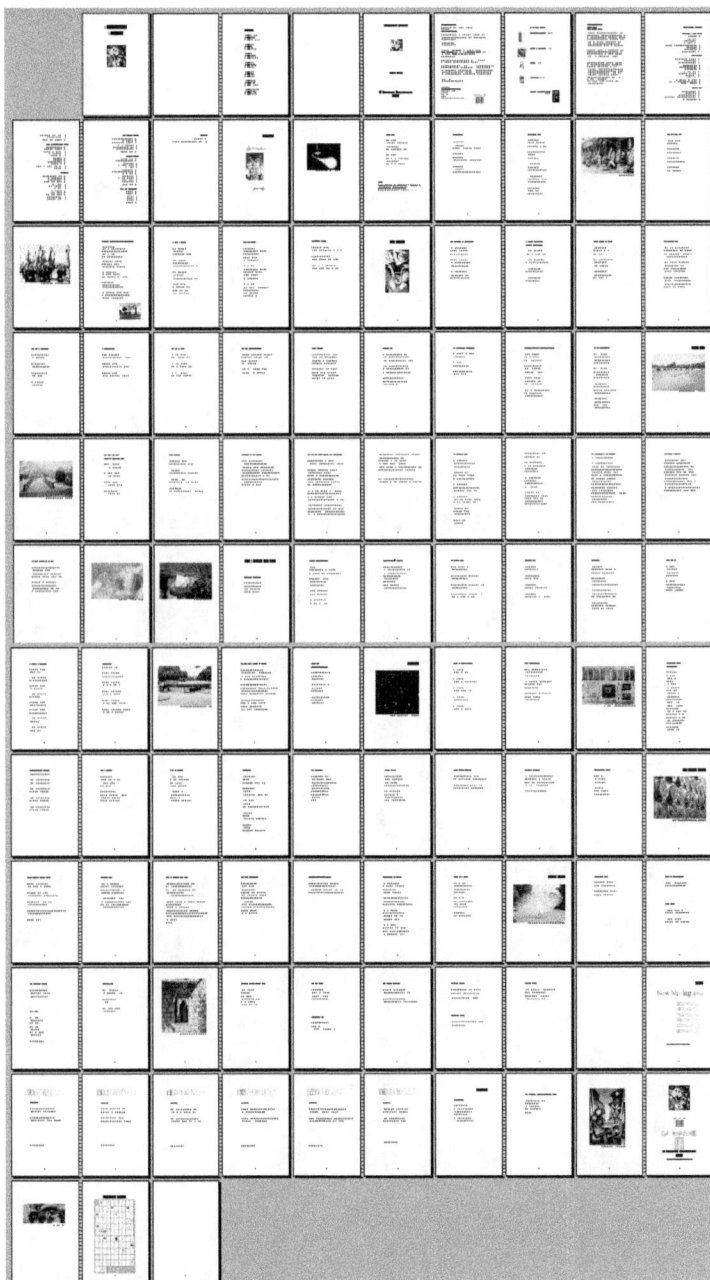

97